W9-CCP-398

BANK STREET
GRAPHIC NOVELS

MURDER & MYSTERY

THE HOUND OF THE BASKERVILLES

Macbeth

THE LEGEND OF SLEEPY HOLLOW

WORLD ALMANAC® LIBRARY

A note from the editors: These stories reflect many of the values, opinions, and standards of language that existed during the times in which the works were written. Much of the language is also a reflection of the personalities and lifestyles of the stories' narrators and characters. Readers today may strongly disagree, for example, with the ways in which members of various groups, such as women or ethnic minorities, are described or portrayed. In compiling these works, however, we felt that it was important to capture as much of the flavor and character of the original stories as we could and to use art that also captures the spirit of the lives and times of the stories and characters. Rather than delete or alter language that is intrinsically important to literature, we hope that these stories will give parents, educators, and young readers a chance to think and talk about the many ways in which people lead their lives, view the world, and express their feelings about what they have lived through.

Please visit our Web site at: www.garethstevens.com
For a free color catalog describing World Almanac® Library's
list of high-quality books and multimedia programs,
call 1-800-848-2928 (USA) or 1-800-387-3178 (Canada).
World Almanac® Library's fax: (414) 332-3567.

Library of Congress Cataloging-in-Publication Data available upon request from publisher.
Fax (414) 336-0157 for the attention of the Publishing Records Department.

ISBN-13: 978-0-8368-7928-5 (lib. bdg.)
ISBN-13: 978-0-8368-7935-3 (softcover)

This North American edition first published in 2007 by
World Almanac® Library
A Member of the WRC Media Family of Companies
330 West Olive Street, Suite 100
Milwaukee, Wisconsin 53212 USA

"The Hound of the Baskervilles" adapted by Shannon Lowry, illustrated by Mike Vosburg from *The Hound of the Baskervilles* by Sir Arthur Conan Doyle. Copyright © 2001 by Bank Street College of Education. Created in collaboration with *Boys' Life* magazine. First published in *Boys' Life* magazine, November 2001, by the Boy Scouts of America. Reprinted by permission of Bank Street College of Education and *Boys' Life* magazine.

"William Shakespeare's Macbeth" adapted by Suzette Haden Elgin, art by Mike Vosburg from *Macbeth* by William Shakespeare. Copyright © 2001 by Bank Street College of Education. Created in collaboration with *Boys' Life* magazine. First published in *Boys' Life* magazine, May 2001, by the Boy Scouts of America. Reprinted by permission of Bank Street College of Education and *Boys' Life* magazine.

"The Legend of Sleepy Hollow" adapted by Shannon Lowry, illustrated by Dan Spiegle from *The Legend of Sleepy Hollow* by Washington Irving. Copyright © 2000 by Bank Street College of Education. Created in collaboration with *Boys' Life* magazine. First published in *Boys' Life* magazine, October 2000, by the Boy Scouts of America. Reprinted by permission of Bank Street College of Education and *Boys' Life* magazine.

This U.S. edition copyright © 2007 by World Almanac® Library.

World Almanac® Library editorial direction: Mark Sachner
World Almanac® Library editors: Monica Rausch and Tea Benduhn
World Almanac® Library art direction: Tammy West
World Almanac® Library designer: Scott Krall
World Almanac® Library production: Jessica Yanke and Robert Kraus

Printed in Canada

1 2 3 4 5 6 7 8 9 10 10 09 08 07 06

THE HOUND OF THE BASKERVILLES

PAGES 4-20

PAGES 22-38

THE LEGEND OF SLEEPY

PAGES 40-56

THE HOUND OF THE BASKERVILLES

BY SIR ARTHUR CONAN DOYLE

ADAPTED BY
SHANNON LOWRY

ILLUSTRATIONS BY
MIKE VOSBURG

DEVONSHIRE, ENGLAND, 1889. THE CURSE OF THE BASKERVILLES HAD STRUCK AGAIN! SIR CHARLES BASKERVILLE WAS FOUND DEAD NEAR HIS ESTATE. THOUGH NO ONE WITNESSED THE TERRIBLE SCENE, PEOPLE REPORTED HEARING THE HORRIBLE HOWL OF A HOUND.

THIS MYSTERY SOON CAME TO THE ATTENTION OF THE GREAT DETECTIVE, SHERLOCK HOLMES, AND HIS FRIEND, DR. WATSON, IN LONDON.

COLORS AND LETTERING BY JOHN OTT

SIR ARTHUR CONAN DOYLE

SIR ARTHUR CONAN DOYLE WAS BORN ON MAY 22, 1959, TO IRISH PARENTS IN EDINBURGH, SCOTLAND. HIS MOTHER WAS A GREAT STORYTELLER, AND HE GREW UP LISTENING TO HER TALES. WHILE IN SCHOOL, DOYLE FASCINATED FRIENDS WITH HIS OWN STORIES. HE LATER WENT TO MEDICAL SCHOOL AND BECAME A DOCTOR. IN BETWEEN PATIENT VISITS, DOYLE BEGAN WRITING. HE PUBLISHED A FEW SHORT STORIES BEFORE WRITING THE NOVEL **A STUDY IN SCARLET**, IN WHICH HE INTRODUCED THE CHARACTER SHERLOCK HOLMES, IN 1887. THE CHARACTER, WITH HIS LOGIC AND DEDUCTIVE REASONING, WAS SAID TO BE BASED ON A TEACHER DOYLE HAD HAD IN MEDICAL SCHOOL. HOLMES BECAME AN INSTANT FAVORITE AMONG READERS, BUT DESPITE HIS POPULARITY, DOYLE GREW TIRED OF WRITING ABOUT HIM. IN 1893, DOYLE HAD HIM DIE IN THE STORY "THE FINAL PROBLEM." READERS, HOWEVER, WERE UPSET BY THE DEATH. DOYLE THEN WROTE **THE HOUND OF THE BASKERVILLES** IN 1902 AS A TALE THAT OCCURRED BEFORE HOLMES'S DEATH. IN 1903, HE WROTE "THE EMPTY HOUSE," IN WHICH HOLMES REAPPEARED. THE STORY EXPLAINED THAT HOLMES HAD FAKED HIS DEATH TO AVOID HIS

Macbeth

PAGES 22-38

THE LEGEND OF

A BANK STREET CLASSIC TALE

William Shakespeare's Macbeth

Adapted by Suzette Haden Elgin
Art by Mike Vosburg

CLANG! CLANG!

THUNK

This was how the wicked plan of Macbeth and Lady Macbeth ended—in defeat and death. It was as all that is wicked must end.

HAIL TO YOU, *MALCOLM!* HAIL, KING OF SCOTLAND!

HAIL, KING OF SCOTLAND!

the end

The year is 1608: William Shakespeare (1564–1616) directs actors in a rehearsal of his new play "Macbeth" at the Globe Theater in London, England. England, ruled by Queen Elizabeth I, is a world superpower. Shakespeare wrote at least one play performed at her court.

The Globe Theater was torn down in 1644 but rebuilt in 1997. Today the new Globe Theater features plays by Shakespeare and other writers.

ACT V

WILLIAM SHAKESPEARE

WILLIAM SHAKESPEARE WAS A WELL-KNOWN BRITISH POET, PLAYWRIGHT, AND ACTOR DURING THE LATE 1500S AND EARLY 1600S. SHAKESPEARE WAS BORN IN 1564 IN STRATFORD, ENGLAND. THE ACTUAL DATE OF HIS BIRTH IS NOT KNOWN, BUT APRIL 23, THREE DAYS BEFORE HIS BAPTISM, IS THE DATE MANY PEOPLE CELEBRATE AS HIS BIRTHDAY. DETAILS OF HIS LIFE ARE MUCH DEBATED, BUT HE PROBABLY WAS ENROLLED IN A GRAMMAR SCHOOL THAT TAUGHT THE LATIN LANGUAGE AND HISTORY AND PERHAPS OFFERED CLASSES IN THEATER AND ACTING. HE MARRIED ANNE HATHAWAY IN 1582, WHEN HE WAS JUST EIGHTEEN. THEY HAD THREE CHILDREN TOGETHER. LATER, HE BEGAN WORKING IN THEATERS IN LONDON, WRITING POEMS AND PLAYS, AND ACTING IN THEATER PRODUCTIONS. HE EVENTUALLY BECAME ASSOCIATED WITH A THEATER GROUP CALLED THE KING'S MEN, WHICH BOUGHT AND PERFORMED HIS PLAYS. THE GROUP PERFORMED PLAYS FOR THE ROYAL COURT AS WELL AS FOR THE PUBLIC, AND SHAKESPEARE'S PLAYS BECAME VERY POPULAR. HE EVENTUALLY BOUGHT SEVERAL THEATERS FOR PUTTING ON PLAYS. SHAKESPEARE DIED ON APRIL 23, 1616. VERY FEW OF HIS PLAYS WERE PUBLISHED DURING HIS LIFETIME, BUT MANY OF HIS PLAYS WERE COLLECTED AND PUBLISHED AFTER HIS DEATH, IN 1623. MACBETH WAS WRITTEN AND PERFORMED IN THE EARLY 1600S. OTHER PLAYS INCLUDE ROMEO AND JULIET, A MIDSUMMER NIGHT'S DREAM, HAMLET, AND KING LEAR. PEOPLE STILL DO NOT KNOW EXACTLY HOW MANY PLAYS AND POEMS HE WROTE.

THE HOUND OF THE BASKERVILLES

PAGES 4–20

Macbeth

PAGES 22–38

A BANK STREET CLASSIC TALE

THE LEGEND OF SLEEPY HOLLOW

PAGES 40–56

THE LEGEND OF SLEEPY HOLLOW

By Washington Irving

Adapted by Shannon Lowry
Illustrated by Dan Spiegle

IN NEW YORK STATE NEAR THE EASTERN SHORE OF THE HUDSON RIVER IS SLEEPY HOLLOW, A QUIET VALLEY STRANGELY FULL OF HAUNTED SPOTS AND GHOSTS. THE MOST TERRIFYING ONE IS A FIGURE ON HORSEBACK, WITHOUT A HEAD.

THE *HEADLESS HORSEMAN* IS THE GHOST OF A HESSIAN TROOPER. A CANNONBALL SHOT OFF HIS HEAD DURING THE REVOLUTIONARY WAR.

LEGEND HAS IT THAT HIS GHOST RIDES TO THE BATTLE SCENE EVERY NIGHT TO LOOK FOR HIS HEAD!

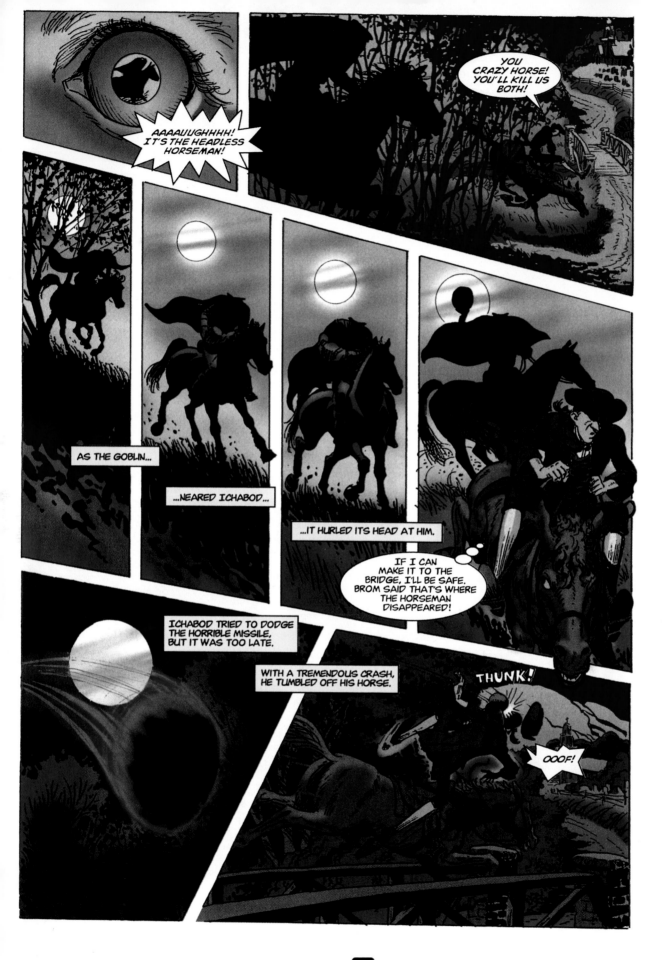

WASHINGTON IRVING

WASHINGTON IRVING WAS BORN ON APRIL 3, 1783, IN NEW YORK CITY, AT THE END OF THE AMERICAN REVOLUTION. HIS PARENTS NAMED HIM AFTER THE AMERICAN WAR HERO GEORGE WASHINGTON. AS A BOY, IRVING READ MANY ADVENTURE STORIES, AND HE LATER STUDIED LAW. HE TRAVELED TO EUROPE IN THE EARLY 1800S AND THEN BEGAN WORKING FOR HIS FATHER'S BUSINESS. HE ALSO STARTED WRITING ESSAYS AND COLUMNS FOR HIS BROTHER'S NEWSPAPER. IN 1809, HE PUBLISHED **A HISTORY OF NEW YORK**, A HUMOROUS ACCOUNT OF THE EARLY DUTCH SETTLERS OF NEW YORK THAT IRVING WROTE UNDER THE NAME OF HIS FICTIONAL CHARACTER, DIEDRICH KNICKERBOCKER. THE BOOK WAS A SUCCESS, AND THE TERM "KNICKERBOCKER" SOON BECAME A POPULAR NAME FOR ANYONE OF DUTCH ANCESTRY IN NEW YORK. HIS NEXT BOOK WAS A COLLECTION OF SHORT STORIES CALLED **THE SKETCHBOOK OF GEOFFREY CRAYON, GENT** (1819). "THE LEGEND OF SLEEPY HOLLOW" AND "RIP VAN WINKLE" WERE TWO OF THE BEST-KNOWN STORIES IN THAT COLLECTION. THE STORIES WERE OFTEN BASED ON GERMAN FOLK TALES BUT SET IN THE UNITED STATES. THE DESCRIPTION OF SLEEPY HOLLOW IS BELIEVED TO BE TAKEN FROM THE HUDSON RIVER VALLEY, NEAR TARRYTOWN, NEW YORK, WHERE IRVING LIVED WHEN HE WASN'T TRAVELING. IRVING EVENTUALLY WAS ABLE TO WRITE FOR A LIVING, BECOMING THE FIRST AMERICAN TO DO SO. HE SPENT HIS TIME WRITING AND TRAVELING THROUGH EUROPE AND IN THE AMERICAN WEST. MANY OF HIS LATER WORKS WERE HISTORY BOOKS, INCLUDING **THE LIFE AND VOYAGES OF CHRISTOPHER COLUMBUS** (1828) AND **THE LIFE OF GEORGE WASHINGTON** (1855-1859), A BIOGRAPHY OF HIS NAMESAKE. DURING HIS LATER YEARS, IRVING LIVED IN TARRYTOWN. HE NEVER MARRIED, AND HE DIED ON NOVEMBER 28, 1859.